SPORTS SUPERSTARS

MIKE TROUT

By Anthony K. Hewson

Kaleidoscope
Minneapolis, MN

Your Front Row Seat to the Games

This edition is co-published by agreement between Kaleidoscope and World Book, Inc.

Kaleidoscope Publishing, Inc.
6012 Blue Circle Drive
Minnetonka, MN 55343 U.S.A.

World Book, Inc.
180 North LaSalle St., Suite 900
Chicago IL 60601 U.S.A.

Kaleidoscope ISBNs
978-1-64519-043-1 (library bound)
978-1-64494-200-0 (paperback)
978-1-64519-144-5 (ebook)

World Book ISBN
978-0-7166-4347-0 (library bound)

Library of Congress Control Number
2019940062

Printed in the United States of America.

TABLE OF CONTENTS

CHAPTER 1

Taking Flight

Mike Trout adjusted his cap. He looked over the **diamond** from center field. It was the bottom of the first inning. Trout's Los Angeles Angels were in Baltimore, Maryland. Orioles hitter J. J. Hardy was at the plate. When Hardy's bat made contact with the ball, Trout took off running.

He knew this was a big game. His Angels were playing well in the 2012 season. But so were the Orioles. It was late June. The **wild-card** race was going to be close. The Angels and Orioles were neck-and-neck. Trout knew he had to make a play.

Mike Trout emerged as a star during the 2012 season.

Trout robs J. J. Hardy of a home run.

Trout sprinted to his left. The ball was going over the wall in right-center field. Only Trout could stop it. He never took his eyes off the ball. Once he got to the wall, he jumped. He reached his glove out as far as he could. Then he snatched the ball.

Trout raised his glove in celebration. He yelled and pounded his chest. Angels pitcher Jered Weaver tipped his cap to thank Trout. The Angels had survived a major scare.

FUN FACT

At 21, Trout became the youngest American League (AL) Rookie of the Year.

But Trout was far from done in the game. He also got four hits and drove in a run. The Angels crushed the Orioles 13–1. It was Trout's first full season. He was already a star. He could do everything on the field. Major League Baseball (MLB) fans were taking notice. But Trout's journey was not easy. It took him a lot of hard work to get there.

Trout and his teammates celebrate the win over Baltimore.

CAREER STATS

Through the 2018 season

BATTING AVERAGE	.307
HITS	1,187
HOME RUNS	240
RUNS BATTED IN (RBIs)	648
STOLEN BASES	189

CHAPTER 2

The Millville Meteor

The boy could hit. Everyone in Millville, New Jersey, could see it. Mike Trout had been a little league star. Now he was moving up. High school baseball would be his biggest challenge yet.

Mike was a small kid. Other kids were bigger and stronger, but Mike was fast. At his tryout, Mike was nervous. His heart raced as he worked on infield drills. Again and again he missed throws. Mike cringed as his throws sailed to the backstop.

Coaches wondered if he was good enough. The **varsity** team might have to wait. Maybe he needed time on the **freshman** team first. But Mike turned it around. He showed the coaches what he could do. Mike made varsity. And the rest is history.

Mike was born on August 7, 1991. Baseball was a natural fit.

Mike showed a knack for baseball at a young age.

Where Trout Has Been

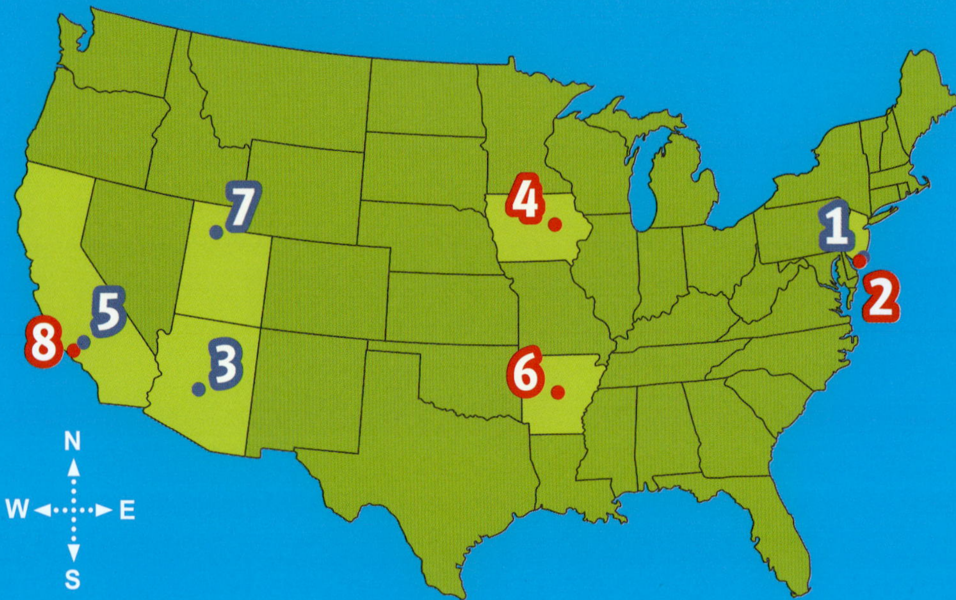

1 **Vineland, New Jersey:** Trout's birthplace.

2 **Millville, New Jersey:** Trout grew up here.

3 **Tempe, Arizona:** Home of the Arizona Angels, where Trout began his pro baseball career.

4 **Cedar Rapids, Iowa:** Home of the Cedar Rapids Kernels, where Trout played Class-A ball.

5 **Rancho Cucamonga, California:** Home of the Rancho Cucamonga Quakes, where Trout played high Class-A ball.

6 **North Little Rock, Arkansas:** Home of the Arkansas Travelers, where Trout played Double-A ball.

7 **Salt Lake City, Utah:** Home of the Salt Lake Bees, where Trout played Triple-A ball.

8 **Anaheim, California:** Home of Trout's team, the Angels.

His father, Jeff, had played in the **minor leagues**. But Jeff never pressured his son in the sport. Mike played to have fun. Maybe baseball could help Mike get into college. But if he had a bad game? No big deal. Jeff and Mike went fishing or got ice cream.

Mike's skill became obvious, though. Jeff had set a lot of records at Millville High School. Mike started breaking them. Even MLB **scouts** took notice.

Greg Morhardt had been Jeff's teammate.

Mike was eager to prove himself in the majors.

Mike poses with MLB Commissioner Bud Selig after being drafted in 2009.

Now he was a scout for the Angels. One day he watched Mike. Morhardt saw Jeff's skills in Mike. But Mike was even better. He reminded Morhardt of one of baseball's all-time greats.

"I think I've got Mickey Mantle up here," Morhardt told the team. "Wait 'til you see this one." Mantle was one of the best players ever.

The Angels wanted Mike. But they were not sure they could get him in the **draft**. Many expected Mike to go before their turn to pick.

Mike was invited to attend the draft. He was not one of the first picks. He waited. He waited some more. Finally, Mike heard his name. The Angels took him with the 25th pick in the first round. Mike was not upset. He could not wait to show the other teams what they missed.

"I looked at it as an opportunity to try and prove some teams wrong," he said.

FUN FACT

Mike once threw a no-hitter while in high school.

CHAPTER 3

Big Fish

It was Christmas Eve in 2015. Many families in Buena Vista Township, New Jersey, were gathering around their trees. For them, it was a joyful time. But that was not the case for the DeSimone family. A fire had destroyed their house a few days earlier. They lost everything.

Buena Vista Township is very close to where Trout grew up. He heard about what the DeSimones were going through. On Christmas Eve, he paid them a visit. He brought some gifts to brighten up their holiday.

"(Trout) remembers where he came from, and he really helps the people in this area," said Tony DeSimone.

Trout hoped Christmas presents could help lift the DeSimone family's spirits.

Trout signs an autograph for a fan.

FUN FACT

Trout's favorite restaurant meal back in Millville is six small hamburgers with no cheese.

FAMOUS FRIENDS

Trout grew up near Philadelphia, Pennsylvania. As a kid he cheered for the Philadelphia Eagles football team. Trout is still a huge Eagles fan. He got to know Eagles quarterback Carson Wentz. They became friends. Trout and Wentz like to spend time together in the offseason.

Home means a lot to Trout. Just take a look around Millville. Signs welcome visitors to the "home of Mike Trout." The high school baseball field is Mike Trout Field. He loves the town. The town loves him back.

In 2014, Trout signed a new **contract** with the Angels. It paid him $144.5 million over six years. But he did not buy a fancy house. He kept living with his parents back home. It was just where he felt comfortable.

"He's a family guy," his dad said. "He loves his (three-legged) dog. He's close with his mother. He has a great group of friends here he's had since he was a little kid."

Trout finally moved out in 2016. But he still comes home to spend time with friends. He loves the outdoors. He and his friends like to hunt and fish.

During the season, Trout lives in Los Angeles. It is the picture of paradise. But Trout is no Hollywood celebrity. He lives a quiet life with his wife and dog. He has known his wife, Jessica, since they were in high school.

"Obviously, baseball is great and all," Trout said. "But once the game is over, you want to be yourself. You want to be a regular guy."

Trout, center, poses with family and members of the Angels staff.

CHAPTER 4

Becoming the MVP

The summer air was hot. Fans settled into their seats. It was a perfect night for baseball in Cincinnati, Ohio. But this was no ordinary game. It was the 2015 All-Star Game.

Trout slides safely into home plate at the 2015 All-Star Game.

There was a special buzz in the air. And Mike Trout was the first batter for his team.

Angels teammate Albert Pujols had some advice. He told Trout that he should swing at the first pitch.

Trout makes a diving catch in the outfield.

Trout was not that aggressive. He took the first pitch for a strike. He fouled off the next one. Then he took a ball. Now Trout was dialed in.

He hammered the next pitch to right field. Right fielder Bryce Harper looked. But that was all he could do as the ball sailed into the seats. Trout and the AL team won 6–3. Trout won the game's Most Valuable Player (MVP) Award.

By then, everyone knew Trout. He was one of baseball's biggest stars.

FUN FACT

Trout scored in 15 straight games in 2012. That set an Angels record.

In fact, the All-Star Game MVP Award was his second in a row.

"I've got the best seat every day, playing with him," Pujols said.

It was not an easy journey. Trout hit just .220 in 40 games in 2011. He got sent back down to the minor leagues. But he was only 19 years old. He trusted himself. He trusted his skills.

"I am working through it," he said. "Working hard every day at it."

Trout was back with the Angels in 2012. He was a new player. Trout could hit the ball all over the park. He was fast, too. Plus, Trout could make crazy catches. In 2014, he was named AL MVP. He won it again in 2016. Four other times he was runner-up.

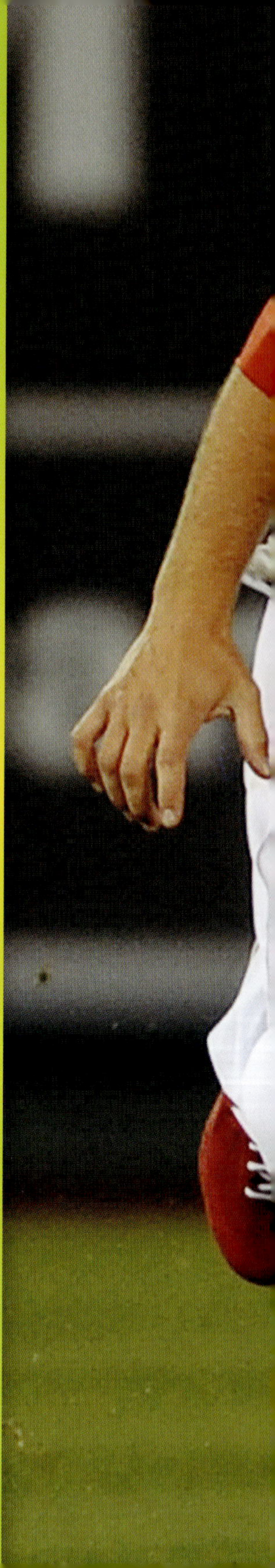

Trout makes a running catch during his 2014 MVP season.

On June 21, 2018, Trout played his 1,000th career game. He walked three times and scored two runs. But oddly he did not record a hit. In his career, he had 1,126 hits. That was only five fewer than Pete Rose had at that age. Rose later became the all-time hits leader in MLB. And Trout was right there.

But he never thinks that far ahead.

"For me, I just have fun going to the ballpark," Trout said. "I just want to be the best every day."

Trout has already had much to celebrate in his career.

CAREER TIMELINE

1991

August 7, 1991
Trout is born in Vineland, New Jersey.

2009

June 2009
Trout is drafted 25th overall by the Los Angeles Angels.

2009

2009
Trout makes his pro baseball debut with the minor league Arizona Angels.

2011

July 8, 2011
Trout makes his major league debut.

2011

July 9, 2011
Trout gets his first major league hit, a single against the Seattle Mariners.

2012

2012
Trout hits .326 with 30 home runs and 83 RBIs as he wins AL Rookie of the Year.

2014

2014
Trout hits 36 home runs and leads the AL in RBIs, winning the AL MVP Award.

2016

2016
Trout wins his second MVP Award.

2019

March 20, 2019
Trout agrees to a new 12-year contract with the Angels that will pay him a record $430 million.

BEYOND THE BOOK

After reading the book, it's time to think about what you learned. Try the following exercises to jumpstart your ideas.

THINK

THAT'S NEWS TO ME. Chapter Four describes Trout hitting a home run to lead off the All-Star Game. This event was covered by the news. What other information do you think news sources could provide about this game? Where would you go to find those sources?

CREATE

PRIMARY SOURCES. A primary source is a source that contains firsthand information. That means it comes directly from the people who lived through the event. What would primary sources about Trout look like? Create a list of some ideas.

SHARE

SUM IT UP. Write a paragraph that summarizes this entire book. Be sure to use your own words; don't recycle any text from the book. Share your paragraph with a classmate. What did your classmate think? Was there any feedback? Did he or she have any questions?

GROW

REAL-LIFE RESEARCH. You can learn a lot about Trout by reading about him. But what places could you visit to learn more about him? What other topics could be explored at these places?

RESEARCH NINJA

Visit *www.ninjaresearcher.com/0431* to learn how to take your research skills and book report writing to the next level!

RESEARCH

DIGITAL LITERACY TOOLS

SEARCH LIKE A PRO
Learn about how to use search engines to find useful websites.

FACT OR FAKE?
Discover how you can tell a trusted website from an untrustworthy resource.

TEXT DETECTIVE
Explore how to zero in on the information you need most.

SHOW YOUR WORK
Research responsibly—learn how to cite sources.

WRITE

GET TO THE POINT
Learn how to express your main ideas.

PLAN OF ATTACK
Learn prewriting exercises and create an outline.

DOWNLOADABLE REPORT FORMS

Further Resources

BOOKS

Buckley, Conor. *Los Angeles Angels.* The Child's World, 2019.

Hoblin, Paul. *Mike Trout.* Abdo Publishing, 2016.

Wilson, Bernie. *Los Angeles Angels.* Abdo Publishing, 2015.

WEBSITES

FACTSURFER

Factsurfer.com gives you a safe, fun way to find more information.

1. Go to www.factsurfer.com.
2. Enter "Mike Trout" into the search box and click .
3. Select your book cover to see a list of related websites.

Glossary

contract: A contract is a legal agreement in which a player and team agree to work together. Trout signed a new contract in 2014.

diamond: The diamond is a nickname for a baseball field due to its shape. The Angels took their positions on the diamond to start the game.

draft: The draft is an event in which baseball teams select new players who are entering the league. Trout was chosen 25th in the draft.

freshman: A freshman is a first-year student in high school or college. Trout made the varsity team as a high school freshman.

minor leagues: Minor leagues are the levels underneath the major leagues where players develop their skills. Trout played in the minor leagues before making it to MLB.

scouts: Scouts are trained professionals who evaluate players. Scouts liked what they saw from Trout.

varsity: A high school's varsity team is its best team in that sport. Trout played varsity baseball in high school.

wild card: A wild card is a team that qualifies for the playoffs without winning its division. The Angels finished second in their division but still made the playoffs as a wild-card team.

Index

PHOTO CREDITS

The images in this book are reproduced through the courtesy of: Ric Tapia/Icon Sportswire/AP Images, front cover (center); Brian Rothmuller/Icon Sportswire/AP Images, front cover (right), p.3; Marcio Jose Bastos Silva/Shutterstock Images, front cover (background); Dan Thornberg/Shutterstock Images, pp. 4, 27 (ball); Charlie Neibergall/AP Images, pp. 4–5; Nick Wass/AP Images, pp. 6–7, 8; Leslie Plaza Johnson/Icon Sportswire/AP Images, p. 9 (Mike Trout); Red Line Editorial, pp. 9 (chart), 12, 27 (timeline); J. McPhail/Shutterstock Images, pp. 10–11; Alexander Lukatskiy/Shutterstock Images, p. 11; Debby Wong/Shutterstock Images, p. 13; Rich Schultz/AP Images, p. 14; fotohunter/Shutterstock Images, p. 16; Alex Gallardo/AP Images, p. 17; Chris Williams/Icon Sportswire/AP Images, p. 18; 104000/Shutterstock Images, p. 20; Jeff Roberson/AP Images, pp. 20–21; Mark J. Terrill/AP Images, pp. 22–23; John Cordes/Icon Sportswire via AP Images, pp. 24–25; Matt Marton/AP Images, p. 26; Andrey_Popov/Shutterstock Images, pp. 27 (glove), 30.

ABOUT THE AUTHOR

Anthony K. Hewson is a freelance writer originally from San Diego, now living in the Bay Area with his wife and their two dogs.